KITCHEN LIBRARY
# One Pot

*p*

# gardener's broth

### serves six

40 g/1½ oz butter

1 onion, chopped

1–2 garlic cloves, crushed

1 large leek

225 g/8 oz Brussels sprouts

125 g/4½ oz French or runner beans

1.2 litres/2 pints vegetable stock

125 g/4½ oz frozen peas

1 tbsp lemon juice

½ tsp ground coriander

4 tbsp double cream

salt and pepper

MELBA TOAST

4–6 slices white bread

1 Melt the butter in a pan over a low heat. Add the onion and garlic and fry for 2–3 minutes, or until they start to soften, but not colour.

2 Slice the white part of the leek very thinly and reserve. Slice the remaining leek, then slice the Brussels sprouts and thinly slice the beans.

3 Add the green part of the leeks, the Brussels sprouts and beans to the pan. Add the stock and bring to the boil over a medium heat, then reduce the heat and simmer for 10 minutes.

4 Add the peas and seasoning. Add the lemon juice and ground coriander. Cook for 10–15 minutes, or until the vegetables are tender.

5 Leave the soup to cool slightly, then transfer to a food processor and process until smooth. Alternatively, rub through a sieve with the back of a spoon. Pour into a clean pan.

6 Add the reserved slices of leek to the soup, bring back to the boil and cook for about 5 minutes until the leek is tender. Adjust the seasoning, stir in the cream and heat through.

7 To make the Melba toast, toast the bread on both sides under a preheated hot grill. Cut horizontally through the slices, then toast the uncooked sides until they curl up. Serve immediately with the soup.

# chick-pea soup

## serves four

2 tbsp olive oil

2 leeks, sliced

2 courgettes, diced

2 garlic cloves, crushed

800 g/1 lb 12 oz canned
chopped tomatoes

1 tbsp tomato purée

1 fresh bay leaf

850 ml/1½ pints vegetable stock

400 g/14 oz canned chick-peas,
drained and rinsed

225 g/8 oz spinach

salt and pepper

TO SERVE

freshly grated Parmesan cheese

warmed sun-dried tomato bread

1 Heat the oil in a large pan over a medium heat. Add the leeks and courgettes and cook briskly for 5 minutes, stirring constantly.

2 Add the crushed garlic, chopped tomatoes, tomato purée, bay leaf, stock and chick-peas.

3 Bring to the boil, then reduce the heat and simmer for 5 minutes.

4 Shred the spinach finely, add to the soup and cook for 2 minutes. Season to taste with salt and pepper.

5 Remove the bay leaf and discard. Ladle the soup into 4 warmed bowls and serve with Parmesan cheese and warmed sun-dried tomato bread.

## COOK'S TIP

Chick-peas are used extensively in North African cuisine and are also found in Spanish, Middle Eastern and Indian cooking. They have a nutty flavour with a firm texture and are excellent canned.

# chicken & pasta broth

## serves six

350 g/12 oz boneless
   chicken breasts
2 tbsp sunflower oil
1 medium onion, diced
250 g/9 oz carrots, diced
250 g/9 oz cauliflower florets
850 ml/1½ pints chicken stock
2 tsp dried mixed herbs
125 g/4½ oz dried pasta shapes
salt and pepper
freshly grated Parmesan
   cheese, optional

### VARIATION

Broccoli florets can be used
to replace the cauliflower
florets, if you prefer. Substitute
2 tbsp of chopped fresh
mixed herbs for the dried
mixed herbs.

1 Remove any skin from the chicken breasts and discard. Finely dice the chicken with a sharp knife.

2 Heat the oil in a large heavy-based pan or frying pan over a medium-high heat. Add the diced chicken, onion, carrots and cauliflower florets, and quickly sauté until they are lightly coloured.

3 Stir in the stock and herbs. Bring to the boil and add the pasta shapes. Return to the boil, cover and simmer for 10 minutes, stirring occasionally to prevent the pasta shapes sticking together.

4 Season to taste with salt and pepper. Sprinkle with the Parmesan cheese (if using) and serve.

# mushroom noodle soup

## serves four

125 g/4½ oz flat or
   open-cup mushrooms
½ cucumber
2 spring onions
1 garlic clove
2 tbsp vegetable oil
600 ml/1 pint water
25 g/1 oz Chinese rice noodles
¾ tsp salt
1 tbsp soy sauce

### COOK'S TIP

Scooping the seeds out from the cucumber gives it a prettier effect when sliced. This also helps to reduce any bitterness, but if you prefer, you can leave them in.

1 Wash the mushrooms and pat dry on kitchen paper. Slice thinly. Do not remove the mushroom peel as this adds more flavour.

2 Cut the cucumber in half lengthways. Taking care not to damage the flesh, scoop out the seeds with a teaspoon, then slice the cucumber thinly and reserve.

3 Chop the spring onions finely and cut the garlic into thin strips.

4 Heat the oil in a large pan or wok over a medium heat.

5 Add the spring onions and garlic to the pan or wok and stir-fry for 30 seconds. Add the mushrooms and stir-fry for a further 2–3 minutes.

6 Stir in the water. Break the noodles into short lengths and add to the soup. Bring to the boil over a medium heat, stirring occasionally.

7 Add the cucumber slices, salt and soy sauce and simmer for about 2–3 minutes.

8 Ladle the mushroom noodle soup into 4 warmed soup bowls, distributing the noodles and vegetables evenly. Serve immediately.

# chunky potato & beef soup

### serves four

2 tbsp vegetable oil

225 g/8 oz lean braising or frying
    steak, cut into strips

225 g/8 oz new potatoes, halved

1 carrot, diced

2 celery sticks, sliced

2 leeks, sliced

850 ml/1½ pints beef stock

8 baby sweetcorn, sliced

1 bouquet garni

2 tbsp dry sherry

salt and pepper

chopped fresh parsley, to garnish

crusty bread, to serve

### COOK'S TIP

Make double quantity of
soup and freeze the remainder
in a rigid container for later use.
When ready to use, leave in the
refrigerator to thaw thoroughly,
then heat until piping hot.

1 Heat the oil in a large pan over a medium heat. Add the strips of steak to the pan and cook for about 3 minutes, turning constantly.

2 Add the potatoes, carrot, celery and leeks. Cook, stirring constantly, for a further 5 minutes.

3 Pour in the stock and bring to the boil over a medium heat. Reduce the heat until the liquid is simmering gently. Add the sliced baby sweetcorn and the bouquet garni.

4 Cook the soup for a further 20 minutes, or until the meat and all the vegetables are tender.

5 Remove the bouquet garni from the pan and discard. Stir the dry sherry into the soup, then season to taste with salt and pepper.

6 Ladle the soup into 4 large, warmed soup bowls and garnish with chopped fresh parsley. Serve immediately with lots of crusty bread.

# umbrian onion soup

## serves four

700 g/1 lb 9 oz onions

115 g/4 oz rindless streaky bacon or
 pancetta, chopped

25 g/1 oz unsalted butter

2 tbsp olive oil

2 tsp sugar

salt and pepper

1.2 litres/2 pints chicken stock

350 g/12 oz plum tomatoes, peeled
 and chopped

12 fresh basil leaves

freshly grated Parmesan cheese,
 to serve

3 Tear 8 of the basil leaves into pieces and stir into the soup, then taste and adjust the seasoning, if necessary. Ladle the soup into warmed bowls, garnish with the remaining basil leaves and serve, handing the Parmesan cheese round separately.

1 Thinly slice the onions and reserve. Place the bacon in a large, heavy-based saucepan and cook over a low heat, stirring, for 5 minutes, or until the fat begins to run. Add the butter, olive oil, sliced onions, sugar and a pinch of salt and stir to mix. Cover and cook, stirring occasionally, for 15–20 minutes, or until the onions are golden brown.

2 Pour in the stock, add the tomatoes and season to taste with salt and pepper. Cover and simmer, stirring occasionally, for 30 minutes.

# chicken & leek soup

## serves six

350 g/12 oz boneless
    chicken breasts
350 g/12 oz leeks
25 g/1 oz butter
1.2 litres/2 pints chicken stock
1 bouquet garni
8 stoned prunes
cooked rice and diced
    peppers, optional
salt and white pepper

---

### VARIATION

Instead of a bouquet garni
sachet, you can use a bunch of
fresh mixed herbs, tied together
with string. Choose herbs such as
parsley, thyme and rosemary.

---

1 Using a sharp knife, cut the
chicken and leeks into 2.5-cm/
1-inch pieces.

2 Melt the butter in a large pan
over a medium heat. Add the
chicken and leeks and sauté for
8 minutes, stirring occasionally.

3 Add the stock and bouquet garni
to the mixture in the pan. Season
to taste with salt and white pepper.

4 Bring the soup to the boil over a
medium heat, then reduce the
heat and simmer for 45 minutes.

5 Add the stoned prunes with some
cooked rice and diced peppers
(if using) and simmer for 20 minutes.
Remove the bouquet garni and
discard. Ladle the soup into a warmed
tureen or serving bowls and serve.

# chicken stir-fry with a trio of peppers

## serves four

450 g/1 lb skinless boneless chicken
    breast portions
2 tbsp sunflower oil
1 garlic clove, crushed
1 tbsp cumin seeds
1 tbsp grated fresh root ginger
1 fresh red chilli, deseeded and sliced
1 red pepper, deseeded and sliced
1 green pepper, deseeded
    and sliced
1 yellow pepper, deseeded
    and sliced
100 g/3½ oz beansprouts
350 g/12 oz pak choi or other
    green leaves
2 tbsp sweet chilli sauce
3 tbsp light soy sauce
deep-fried crispy ginger, to garnish
    (see Cook's Tip)
freshly cooked noodles, to serve

1 Using a sharp knife, slice the chicken into thin strips.

2 Heat the oil in a large preheated wok.

3 Add the chicken to the wok and stir-fry for 5 minutes.

4 Add the garlic, cumin seeds, ginger and chilli to the wok, stirring to mix.

5 Add all of the peppers to the wok and stir-fry for a further 5 minutes.

6 Toss in the beansprouts and pak choi together with the sweet chilli sauce and soy sauce and continue to cook until the pak choi leaves start to wilt.

7 Transfer to serving bowls, garnish with ginger (see Cook's Tip) and serve with freshly cooked noodles.

### COOK'S TIP

To make the deep-fried crispy ginger garnish, peel and thinly slice a large piece of root ginger, using a sharp knife. Carefully lower the slices of ginger into a wok or small pan of hot oil and cook for about 30 seconds. Remove the deep-fried ginger with a slotted spoon, transfer to sheets of absorbent kitchen paper and leave to drain thoroughly.

# braised garlic chicken

## serves four

4 garlic cloves, chopped

4 shallots, chopped

2 small fresh red chillies, deseeded
   and chopped

1 lemon grass stalk, chopped finely

1 tbsp chopped fresh coriander

1 tsp shrimp paste

½ tsp ground cinnamon

1 tbsp tamarind paste

2 tbsp vegetable oil

8 small chicken joints, such as
   drumsticks or thighs

300 ml/10 fl oz chicken stock

1 tbsp Thai fish sauce

1 tbsp smooth peanut butter

4 tbsp toasted peanuts, chopped

salt and pepper

TO SERVE

stir-fried vegetables

freshly cooked noodles

1 Place the garlic, shallots, chillies, lemon grass, coriander and shrimp paste in a mortar and grind with a pestle to an almost smooth paste. Stir in the cinnamon and tamarind paste.

2 Heat the oil in a wok or frying pan. Add the chicken and cook, turning frequently, until golden brown on all sides. Remove with a slotted spoon and keep hot. Tip away any excess fat.

3 Add the garlic paste to the wok or pan and cook over a medium heat, stirring constantly, until lightly browned. Stir in the stock and return the chicken to the wok or pan.

4 Bring to the boil, then cover tightly, lower the heat and simmer, stirring occasionally, for 25–30 minutes, until the chicken is tender and thoroughly cooked. Stir in the fish sauce and peanut butter and simmer gently for a further 10 minutes.

5 Season to taste with salt and pepper and sprinkle the toasted peanuts over the chicken. Serve immediately, with a colourful selection of stir-fried vegetables and freshly cooked noodles.

# chicken cacciatora

## serves four

1 roasting chicken, about 1.5 kg/
    3 lb 5 oz, cut into 6–8
    serving pieces

125 g/4½ oz plain flour

3 tbsp olive oil

150 ml/5 fl oz dry white wine

1 green pepper, deseeded
    and sliced

1 red pepper, deseeded and sliced

1 carrot, chopped finely

1 celery stick, chopped finely

1 garlic clove, crushed

200 g/7 oz canned
    chopped tomatoes

salt and pepper

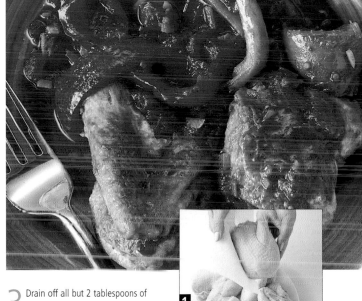

1 Rinse the chicken pieces and pat dry with kitchen paper. Mix the flour and salt and pepper to taste on a plate, then lightly dust the chicken pieces with the seasoned flour.

2 Heat the oil in a large frying pan over a medium heat. Add the chicken and fry until browned all over. Remove from the pan and reserve.

3 Drain off all but 2 tablespoons of the fat in the pan. Add the wine and stir for a few minutes, then add the peppers, carrot, celery and garlic. Season to taste with salt and pepper and simmer together for 15 minutes.

4 Add the chopped tomatoes to the pan. Cover and simmer for 30 minutes, stirring often, until the chicken is completely cooked through.

5 Transfer the chicken and sauce to 4 warmed serving plates and serve immediately.

15

# rich chicken casserole

## serves four

8 chicken thighs

2 tbsp olive oil

1 medium red onion, sliced

2 garlic cloves, crushed

1 large red pepper, sliced thickly

thinly pared rind and juice of
    1 small orange

125 ml/4 fl oz chicken stock

400 g/14 oz canned
    chopped tomatoes

25 g/1 oz sun-dried tomatoes,
    sliced thinly

1 tbsp chopped fresh thyme

50 g/1¾ oz stoned black olives

salt and pepper

crusty bread, to serve

TO GARNISH

orange rind

4 fresh thyme sprigs

### COOK'S TIP

Sun-dried tomatoes have a dense
texture and concentrated taste
and add intense flavour to
slow-cooking casseroles.

1 In a large heavy-based frying pan, fry the chicken without fat over a fairly high heat, turning occasionally, until golden brown. Drain off any excess fat from the chicken with a slotted spoon and transfer to a flameproof casserole dish.

2 Heat the oil in the frying pan over a medium heat. Add the onion, garlic and red pepper and fry for about 3–4 minutes. Transfer the vegetables to the casserole dish.

3 Add the orange rind and juice, stock, chopped tomatoes and sun-dried tomatoes to the casserole and mix well.

4 Bring to the boil, then cover the casserole with a lid and simmer very gently over a low heat for about 1 hour, stirring occasionally. Add the chopped thyme and black olives, then season to taste with salt and pepper.

5 Spoon the chicken casserole on to 4 warmed serving plates, garnish with orange rind and thyme sprigs and serve with crusty bread.

# chicken pepperonata

## serves four

8 skinless chicken thighs

2 tbsp wholemeal flour

2 tbsp olive oil

1 small onion, sliced thinly

1 garlic clove, crushed

1 each large red, yellow and green
    peppers, sliced thinly

400 g/14 oz canned
    chopped tomatoes

1 tbsp chopped fresh oregano

salt and pepper

fresh oregano leaves, to garnish

### COOK'S TIP

If you do not have fresh oregano,
use canned tomatoes with herbs
already added.

1 Remove the skin from the chicken
thighs and toss in the flour.

2 Heat the oil in a frying pan over a
high heat. Add the chicken and
fry until browned. Remove from the
pan. Add the onion and fry until soft.
Add the garlic, peppers, tomatoes and
oregano. Bring to the boil, stirring.

3 Arrange the chicken over the
vegetables. Season well with salt
and pepper, then cover the pan tightly
and simmer for 20–25 minutes, or until
the chicken is tender and the juices run
clear when a skewer is inserted into
the thickest part of the meat.

4 Season to taste, then transfer the
chicken to a large serving dish,
garnish with oregano leaves and serve.

# chicken risotto milanese

### serves four–six

½–1 tsp saffron threads

1.3 litres/2¼ pints chicken
    stock, simmering

85 g/3 oz unsalted butter

2–3 shallots, chopped finely

400 g/14 oz arborio or carnaroli rice

175 g/6 oz freshly grated
    Parmesan cheese

salt and pepper

green salad, to serve

1 Put the saffron threads into a small bowl and pour over enough of the stock to cover the threads, then leave to infuse.

2 Melt 25 g/1 oz of the butter in a large pan over a medium heat. Add the shallots and cook for about 2 minutes, or until starting to soften. Add the rice and cook, stirring frequently, for about 2 minutes, or until the rice is starting to turn translucent and is well coated with the butter.

3 Add a ladleful (about 225 ml/ 8 fl oz) of the simmering stock, it will steam and bubble rapidly. Cook gently, stirring constantly, until all the liquid is absorbed.

4 Continue adding the stock, about half a ladleful at a time, allowing each addition to be completely absorbed before adding the next. Don't allow the rice to cook dry.

5 After about 15 minutes, stir in the saffron-infused stock. The rice will turn a vibrant yellow and the colour will become deeper as it cooks. Continue cooking, adding the stock in the same way until the rice is tender, but still firm to the bite. The risotto should have a creamy consistency.

6 Stir in the remaining butter and half the Parmesan cheese, then remove from the heat. Cover and leave to stand for about 1 minute.

7 Spoon the risotto into large, warmed serving bowls and serve immediately with the remaining Parmesan cheese and a green salad.

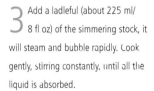

# provençal chicken

## serves four

1.8 kg/4 lb chicken pieces

salt and pepper

1 garlic clove, finely chopped

3 tbsp olive oil

1 onion, finely chopped

225 g/8 oz mushrooms, halved

1 tbsp plain flour

125 ml/4 fl oz chicken stock

175 ml/6 fl oz dry white wine

6 canned anchovy fillets, drained

3 tomatoes, peeled, deseeded and chopped

2 tsp chopped fresh oregano

6 black olives, stoned

**1** Rub the chicken pieces all over with salt, pepper and garlic. Heat the oil in a flameproof casserole. Add the chicken and cook over a medium heat, turning occasionally, for 8–10 minutes, or until golden. Add the onion, cover and cook over a low heat, stirring occasionally, for 20–25 minutes, or until cooked through and tender.

**2** Transfer the chicken to a large serving plate, cover and keep warm. Add the mushrooms to the casserole and cook over a medium heat, stirring constantly, for 3 minutes. Add the flour and cook, stirring constantly, for 1 minute, then gradually stir in the stock and wine. Bring to the boil and cook, stirring, for 10 minutes, or until thickened.

**3** Roughly chop 4 of the anchovies and add them to the casserole with the tomatoes, oregano and olives, then simmer for 5 minutes. Meanwhile, cut the remaining anchovies in half lengthways. Transfer the sauce and chicken to serving plates, garnish with the halved anchovies and serve immediately.

---

**VARIATION**

If you would like a little extra garlic in this dish, crush another clove into the casserole with the stock in Step 2.

---

# coq au vin

## serves four

55 g/2 oz butter

2 tbsp olive oil

1.8 kg/4 lb chicken pieces

115 g/4 oz rindless smoked bacon,
cut into strips

115 g/4 oz baby onions

115 g/4 oz chestnut
mushrooms, halved

2 garlic cloves, finely chopped

2 tbsp brandy

225 ml/8 fl oz red wine

300 ml/10 fl oz chicken stock

1 bouquet garni

salt and pepper

2 tbsp plain flour

bay leaves, to garnish

1 Melt half the butter with the olive oil in a large, flameproof casserole. Add the chicken and cook over a medium heat, stirring, for 8–10 minutes, or until golden brown all over. Add the bacon, onions, mushrooms and garlic.

2 Pour in the brandy and set it alight with a match or taper. When the flames have died down, add the wine, stock and bouquet garni and season to taste with salt and pepper. Bring to the boil, reduce the heat and simmer gently for 1 hour, or until the chicken pieces are cooked through and

tender. Meanwhile, make a beurre manié by mashing the remaining butter with the flour in a small bowl.

3 Remove and discard the bouquet garni. Transfer the chicken to a large plate and keep warm. Stir the beurre manié into the casserole, a little at a time. Bring to the boil, return the chicken to the casserole and serve immediately, garnished with bay leaves.

### VARIATION

You can substitute a good,
full-bodied white wine such as
Chardonnay for the red wine,
if you prefer.

# chicken in white wine

## serves four

2 rindless, thick streaky bacon
    rashers
55 g/2 oz butter
2 tbsp olive oil
115 g/4 oz baby onions
1 garlic clove, finely chopped
1.8 kg/4 lb chicken pieces
400 ml/14 fl oz dry white wine
300 ml/10 fl oz chicken stock
1 bouquet garni
salt and pepper
115 g/4 oz button mushrooms
25 g/1 oz plain flour
fresh mixed herbs, to garnish

1 Preheat the oven to 160°C/325°F/
Gas Mark 3. Peel the baby onions
and prepare the bouquet garni. Chop
the bacon. Melt half the butter with the
oil in a flameproof casserole. Add the
bacon and cook over a medium heat,
stirring, for 5–10 minutes, or until
golden brown. Transfer the bacon to a
large plate. Add the onions and garlic
to the casserole and cook over a low
heat, stirring occasionally, for 10
minutes, or until golden. Transfer to
the plate. Add the chicken and cook
over a medium heat, stirring constantly,
for 8–10 minutes, or until golden.
Transfer to the plate.

2 Drain off any excess fat from the
casserole. Stir in the wine and
stock and bring to the boil, scraping
any sediment off the base. Add
the bouquet garni and season to taste.
Return the bacon, onions and chicken
to the casserole. Cover and cook in the
preheated oven for 1 hour. Add the
mushrooms, re-cover and cook for 15
minutes. Meanwhile, make a beurre
manié by mashing the remaining
butter with the flour in a small bowl.

3 Remove the casserole from the
oven and set over a medium heat.
Remove and discard the bouquet
garni. Whisk in the beurre manié, a
little at a time. Bring to the boil, stirring
constantly, then serve, garnished with
fresh herb sprigs.

---

### VARIATION

If you prefer,
replace the bouquet garni with
1 small bunch of fresh thyme and
garnish the finished dish with
chopped fresh flat-leaved parsley
instead of the mixed herbs.

---

# louisiana chicken

## serves four

5 tbsp sunflower oil

4 chicken portions

55 g/2 oz plain flour

1 onion, chopped

2 celery sticks, sliced

1 green pepper, deseeded and
    chopped

2 garlic cloves, finely chopped

2 tsp chopped fresh thyme

2 fresh red chillies, deseeded
    and finely chopped

400 g/14 oz canned chopped
    tomatoes

300 ml/10 fl oz chicken stock

salt and pepper

TO GARNISH

lamb's lettuce

chopped fresh thyme

---

### VARIATION

Substitute prawns or crayfish for
the chicken. If raw, cook until
they change colour in Step 1 and
return to the casserole near the
end to heat through.

---

**1** Heat the oil in a large, heavy-based saucepan or flameproof casserole. Add the chicken and cook over a medium heat, stirring, for 5–10 minutes, or until golden. Transfer the chicken to a plate with a slotted spoon.

**2** Stir the flour into the oil and cook over a very low heat, stirring constantly, for 15 minutes, or until light golden. Do not let it burn. Immediately, add the onion, celery and green pepper and cook, stirring constantly, for 2 minutes. Add the garlic, thyme and chillies and cook, stirring, for 1 minute.

**3** Stir in the tomatoes and their juices, then gradually stir in the stock. Return the chicken pieces to the saucepan, cover and simmer for 45 minutes, or until the chicken is cooked through and tender. Season to taste with salt and pepper, transfer to warmed serving plates and serve immediately, garnished with some lettuce leaves and a sprinkling of chopped thyme.

# chicken bonne femme

## serves four

1.8 kg/4 lb oven-ready chicken

salt and pepper

55 g/2 oz unsalted butter

675 g/1 lb 8 oz baby onions

675 g/1 lb 8 oz new potatoes

6 rindless bacon rashers, diced

1 bouquet garni

**1** Preheat the oven to 180°C/350°F/ Gas Mark 4. Rinse the chicken inside and out, then pat dry with kitchen paper. Season well with salt and pepper. Melt the butter in a flameproof casserole. Add the chicken and cook over a medium heat, turning frequently, for 8–10 minutes, or until golden. Transfer to a plate.

**2** Add the baby onions, potatoes and bacon to the casserole and cook over a low heat, stirring occasionally, until the onions soften and the potatoes begin to colour.

**3** Return the chicken to the casserole and add the bouquet garni. Cover and cook in the preheated oven for about 1 hour, or until the chicken is cooked through and tender. Remove and discard the bouquet garni. Transfer the chicken to a large serving platter, surround it with the vegetables and bacon and serve immediately.

# chicken & potato bake

## serves four

2 tbsp olive oil

4 lean chicken breasts

bunch of spring onions, trimmed
and chopped

350 g/12 oz young spring carrots,
scrubbed and sliced

125 g/4½ oz French green beans,
trimmed and sliced

600 ml/1 pint chicken stock

350 g/12 oz small new
potatoes, scrubbed

1 small bunch of mixed fresh herbs,
such as thyme, rosemary, bay
and parsley

2 tbsp cornflour

2–3 tbsp cold water

salt and pepper

fresh mixed herb sprigs,
to garnish

1 Heat the oil in a large flameproof
casserole and add the chicken
breasts. Gently fry for 5–8 minutes,
until browned on both sides. Remove
from the casserole with a slotted spoon
and reserve.

2 Add the spring onions, carrots
and green beans and gently fry
for 3–4 minutes.

3 Return the chicken to the
casserole and pour in the stock.
Add the potatoes and herbs. Season,
bring to the boil, then cover the
casserole and transfer to the oven.
Bake in a preheated oven, 190°C/
375°F/Gas Mark 5, for 40–50 minutes,
until the potatoes are tender.

4 Blend the cornflour with the cold
water to a smooth paste. Add to
the casserole, stirring until blended and
thickened. Cover and cook for a further
5 minutes. Garnish with fresh herbs
and serve immediately.

# brunswick stew

## serves six

1.8 kg/4 lb chicken pieces

salt

2 tbsp paprika

2 tbsp olive oil

25 g/1 oz butter

450 g/1 lb onions, chopped

2 yellow peppers, deseeded
  and chopped

400 g/14 oz canned chopped
  tomatoes

225 ml/8 fl oz dry white wine

450 ml/16 fl oz chicken stock

1 tbsp Worcestershire sauce

1/2 tsp Tabasco sauce

1 tbsp finely chopped fresh parsley

325 g/11½ oz canned sweetcorn
  kernels, drained

425 g/15 oz canned butter beans,
  drained and rinsed

2 tbsp plain flour

4 tbsp water

fresh parsley sprigs, to garnish

1 Season the chicken pieces with salt and dust with paprika.

2 Heat the oil and butter in a flameproof casserole or large saucepan. Add the chicken pieces and cook over a medium heat, turning, for 10–15 minutes, or until golden. Transfer to a plate with a slotted spoon.

3 Add the onion and peppers to the casserole. Cook over a low heat, stirring occasionally, for 5 minutes, or until softened. Add the tomatoes,

wine, stock, Worcestershire sauce, Tabasco sauce and parsley and bring to the boil, stirring. Return the chicken to the casserole, cover and simmer, stirring occasionally, for 30 minutes.

4 Add the sweetcorn and beans to the casserole, partially re-cover and simmer for a further 30 minutes. Place the flour and water in a small bowl and mix to make a paste. Stir a ladleful of the cooking liquid into the paste, then stir it into the stew. Cook, stirring frequently, for 5 minutes. Serve, garnished with parsley.

### VARIATION

If you don't have time to make
the chicken stock for this dish,
use water instead, which works
almost as well.

# lamb & potato masala

## serves four

750 g/1 lb 10 oz lean lamb
  (from the leg)
3 tbsp ghee or vegetable oil
500 g/1 lb 2 oz potatoes, peeled
  and cut into large 2.5-cm/
  1-inch pieces
1 large onion, quartered and sliced
2 garlic cloves, peeled
  and crushed
175 g/6 oz mushrooms,
  sliced thickly
280 g/10 oz ready-made Tikka
  Masala Curry Sauce
300 ml/10 fl oz water
3 tomatoes, halved and
  sliced thinly
125g/4½ oz spinach, washed and
  stalks trimmed
salt
fresh mint sprigs, to garnish

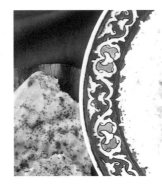

1 Cut the lamb into 2-cm/1-inch cubes. Heat the ghee or oil in a large pan, add the lamb and fry over a medium heat for 3 minutes, or until sealed all over. Remove the lamb from the pan.

2 Add the potatoes, onion, garlic and mushrooms and fry for 3–4 minutes, stirring frequently.

3 Stir the curry sauce and water into the pan, add the lamb, mix well and season with salt to taste. Cover and cook very gently for 1 hour, or until the lamb is tender and cooked through, stirring occasionally.

4 Add the sliced tomatoes and the spinach to the pan, pushing the leaves well down into the mixture, then cover and cook for a further 10 minutes, until the spinach is cooked and tender.

5 Transfer to warmed serving plates, garnish with mint sprigs and serve hot.

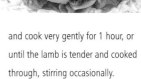

# fruity lamb casserole

## serves four

450 g/1 lb lean lamb, trimmed and
   cut into 2.5-cm/1-inch cubes
1 tsp ground cinnamon
1 tsp ground coriander
1 tsp ground cumin
2 tsp olive oil
1 red onion, chopped finely
1 garlic clove, crushed
400 g/14 oz canned
   chopped tomatoes
2 tbsp tomato purée
125 g/4½ oz no-soak dried apricots
1 tsp caster sugar
300 ml/10 fl oz vegetable stock
salt and pepper
1 small bunch of fresh coriander,
   to garnish
rice or steamed couscous, to serve

1 Place the lamb in a mixing bowl and add the cinnamon, coriander, cumin and oil. Mix thoroughly to coat the lamb in the spices.

2 Place a non-stick frying pan over a high heat for a few seconds until hot, then add the spiced lamb, reduce the heat and cook for 4–5 minutes, stirring, until browned all over. Remove the lamb using a slotted spoon and transfer to a large ovenproof casserole.

3 Add the onion, garlic, tomatoes and tomato purée to the frying pan and cook, stirring occasionally, for 5 minutes. Season to taste with salt and pepper. Stir in the dried apricots and sugar, add the stock and bring to the boil.

4 Spoon the sauce over the lamb and mix well. Cover and cook in a preheated oven, 180°C/350°F/Gas Mark 4, for 1 hour, removing the lid of the casserole for the last 10 minutes.

5 Roughly chop the coriander and sprinkle over the casserole to garnish. Serve immediately with rice or steamed couscous.

# irish stew

## serves four

4 tbsp plain flour

salt and pepper

1.3 kg/3 lb middle neck of lamb,
   trimmed of visible fat

3 large onions, chopped

3 carrots, sliced

450 g/1 lb potatoes, quartered

½ tsp dried thyme

850 ml/1½ pints hot beef stock

2 tbsp chopped fresh parsley,
   to garnish

1 Preheat the oven to 160°C/325°F/
Gas Mark 3. Spread the flour on a
plate and season with salt and pepper.
Roll the pieces of lamb in the flour to
coat, shaking off any excess, and
arrange in the base of a casserole.

2 Layer the onions, carrots and
potatoes on top of the lamb.

3 Sprinkle in the thyme and pour in
the stock, then cover and cook in
the preheated oven for 2½ hours.
Garnish with the chopped fresh parsley
and serve straight from the casserole.

# moroccan lamb

## serves four

500 g/1 lb 2 oz boneless leg of
    lamb

1 tbsp sunflower oil

350 g/12 oz shallots, peeled
    but left whole

425 ml/15 fl oz chicken stock

1 tbsp clear honey

1 tsp ground cinnamon

½ tsp ground ginger

½ tsp saffron threads, lightly
    crushed

¼ tsp freshly grated nutmeg

salt and pepper

grated rind and juice of 1 small
    orange, plus extra rind to garnish

12 no-soak dried prunes

1 Cut the lamb into large cubes.
Heat the oil in a flameproof
casserole, add the lamb and cook over
a medium heat, stirring, for 3–5
minutes, or until browned. Transfer to
a plate. Add the shallots to the
casserole and cook over a low heat,
stirring occasionally, for 10 minutes,
or until golden. Transfer them to a
separate plate with a slotted spoon.

2 Pour away any excess fat from the
casserole, then add the stock and
bring to the boil, stirring constantly and
scraping up any sediment from the
base. Return the lamb to the casserole
and stir in the honey, cinnamon,
ginger, saffron and nutmeg. Season to
taste with salt and pepper, cover and
simmer for 30 minutes.

3 Return the shallots to the casserole
and add the orange rind and juice.
Re-cover and simmer for a further 30

minutes. Add the prunes and adjust
the seasoning, if necessary. Simmer,
uncovered, for a further 15 minutes.
Garnish with orange rind and
serve immediately.

# rogan josh

## serves six

225 ml/8 fl oz natural yogurt

3 tbsp lemon juice

2.5-cm/1-inch piece fresh
    root ginger, grated

2 garlic cloves, finely chopped salt

900 g/2 lb lamb fillet, cut
    into 2.5-cm/1-inch cubes

3 tbsp sunflower oil

½ tsp cumin seeds

4 cardamom pods

1 onion, finely chopped

1 fresh green chilli, deseeded and
    finely chopped

2 tsp ground cumin

2 tsp ground coriander

400 g/14 oz canned chopped
    tomatoes

2 tbsp tomato purée

150 ml/5 fl oz water

2 bay leaves, plus extra to garnish

1 Place the yogurt, lemon juice, ginger and half the garlic in a non-metallic dish and mix. Season well with salt. Add the lamb. Mix well, cover with clingfilm and leave in the refrigerator to marinate for 8 hours or overnight.

2 Heat the oil in a large, heavy-based frying pan over a high heat. Add the cumin seeds and cook, stirring constantly, for 1–2 minutes, or until they begin to pop and release their aroma. Add the cardamom pods and cook, stirring constantly, for a further 2 minutes. Add the onion, chilli and remaining garlic and cook, stirring frequently, for 5 minutes, or until the onion is softened. Stir in the ground cumin and coriander.

3 Add the lamb with the marinade and cook, stirring occasionally, for 5 minutes. Add the tomatoes and their juices, and the tomato purée, water and bay leaves. Bring to the boil, stirring, then reduce the heat, cover and simmer for 1¼–1½ hours, or until cooked through and tender. Garnish with bay leaves and serve.

### VARIATION
Use a red chilli instead of the green chilli if you want the dish to have a slightly sweeter flavour.

# french country casserole

## serves six

2 tbsp sunflower oil

2 kg/4 lb 8 oz boneless leg of lamb, cut into 2.5-cm/1-inch cubes

6 leeks, sliced

1 tbsp plain flour

150 ml/5 fl oz rosé wine

300 ml/10 fl oz chicken stock

1 tbsp tomato purée

1 tbsp sugar

2 tbsp chopped fresh mint

115 g/4 oz dried apricots, chopped

salt and pepper

1 kg/2 lb 4 oz potatoes, sliced

3 tbsp melted unsalted butter

fresh mint sprigs, to garnish

### VARIATION

Use a light red wine instead of rosé if you would prefer a slightly heavier flavour in this country casserole.

1 Preheat the oven to 180°C/350°F/Gas Mark 4. Heat the oil in a large, flameproof casserole. Add the lamb in batches and cook over a medium heat, stirring, for 5–8 minutes, or until browned. Transfer to a plate.

2 Add the sliced leeks to the casserole and cook, stirring occasionally, for 5 minutes, or until softened. Sprinkle in the flour and cook, stirring, for 1 minute. Pour in the wine and stock and bring to the boil, stirring. Stir in the tomato purée, sugar, chopped mint and apricots and season to taste with salt and pepper.

3 Return the lamb to the casserole and stir. Arrange the potato slices on top and brush with the melted

butter. Cover and bake in the preheated oven for 1½ hours.

4 Increase the oven temperature to 200°C/400°F/Gas Mark 6, uncover the casserole and bake for a further 30 minutes, or until the potato topping is golden brown. Serve immediately, garnished with fresh mint sprigs.

# garlic beef with sesame seeds & soy sauce

## serves four

2 tbsp sesame seeds

450 g/1 lb beef fillet

2 tbsp vegetable oil

1 green pepper, deseeded and
    thinly sliced

4 garlic cloves, crushed

2 tbsp dry sherry

4 tbsp dark soy sauce

6 spring onions, sliced

cooked noodles, to serve

### COOK'S TIP

You can spread the sesame
seeds out on a baking tray and
toast them under a preheated
grill until browned all over,
if you prefer.

1 Preheat a large wok or large, heavy-based frying pan until it is very hot.

2 Add the sesame seeds to the wok or frying pan and dry-fry, stirring, for 1–2 minutes, or until they just begin to brown and give off their aroma. Remove the sesame seeds from the wok and reserve until required.

3 Using a sharp knife or meat cleaver, thinly slice the beef.

4 Heat the vegetable oil in the wok or frying pan. Add the beef and stir-fry for 2–3 minutes, or until sealed on all sides.

5 Add the sliced pepper and crushed garlic and continue stir-frying for 2 minutes.

6 Add the dry sherry and soy sauce together with the spring onions. Allow the mixture in the wok or frying pan to bubble, stirring occasionally, for about 1 minute, but do not let it burn.

7 Transfer the garlic beef stir-fry to warm serving bowls and scatter with the dry-fried sesame seeds. Serve hot with noodles.

# beef in beer with herb dumplings

## serves six

### STEW

2 tbsp sunflower oil

2 large onions, thinly sliced

8 carrots, sliced

4 tbsp plain flour

salt and pepper

1.25 kg/2 lb 12 oz stewing steak,
    cut into cubes

425 ml/15 fl oz stout

2 tsp muscovado sugar

2 bay leaves

1 tbsp chopped fresh thyme

### HERB DUMPLINGS

115 g/4 oz self-raising flour

pinch of salt

55 g/2 oz shredded suet

2 tbsp chopped fresh parsley, plus
    extra to garnish

about 4 tbsp water

---

**VARIATION**

Substitute other root vegetables
such as chopped parsnips or
turnips for the sliced carrots,
if you prefer.

---

**1** Preheat the oven to 160°C/325°F/ Gas Mark 3. Heat the oil in a flameproof casserole. Add the onions and carrots and cook over a low heat, stirring occasionally, for 5 minutes, or until the onions are softened. Meanwhile, place the flour in a polythene bag and season with salt and pepper. Add the stewing steak to the bag, tie the top and shake well to coat. Do this in batches, if necessary.

**2** Remove the vegetables from the casserole with a slotted spoon and reserve. Add the stewing steak to the casserole, in batches, and cook, stirring frequently, until browned all over. Return all the meat and the onions and carrots to the casserole and sprinkle in any remaining seasoned flour. Pour in the stout and add the sugar, bay leaves and thyme. Bring to the boil, cover and transfer to the preheated oven to bake for 1¾ hours.

**3** To make the herb dumplings, sift the flour and salt into a bowl. Stir in the suet and parsley and add

enough of the water to make a soft dough. Shape into small balls between the palms of your hands. Add to the casserole and return to the oven for 30 minutes. Remove and discard the bay leaves. Serve immediately, sprinkled with chopped parsley.

# chilli con carne

## serves four

2 tbsp sunflower oil

500 g/1 lb 2 oz fresh beef mince

1 large onion, chopped

1 garlic clove, finely chopped

1 green pepper, deseeded and diced

1 tsp chilli powder

800 g/1 lb 12 oz canned
    chopped tomatoes

800 g/1 lb 12 oz canned red kidney
    beans, drained and rinsed

450 ml/16 fl oz beef stock

salt

handful of fresh coriander sprigs

2 tbsp soured cream, to serve

**1** Heat the oil in a large, heavy-based saucepan or flameproof casserole. Add the beef. Cook over a medium heat, stirring frequently, for 5 minutes, or until broken up and browned.

**2** Reduce the heat, add the onion, garlic and pepper and cook, stirring frequently, for 10 minutes.

**3** Stir in the chilli powder, tomatoes and their juices and kidney beans. Pour in the stock and season with salt.

Bring to the boil, reduce the heat and simmer, stirring frequently, for 15–20 minutes, or until the meat is tender.

**4** Chop the coriander sprigs, reserving a few for a garnish, and stir into the chilli. Adjust the seasoning, if necessary. Either serve immediately with a splash of soured cream, and coriander sprigs to garnish, or leave to cool, then store in the refrigerator overnight. Reheating it the next day makes it more flavoursome.

---

### VARIATION

Substitute 1–2 finely chopped, deseeded fresh chillies for the chilli powder in Step 2. Anaheim (mild) or jalapeño (hot) are classic Tex-Mex varieties.

# simple savoury mince

## serves four

2 tbsp groundnut or sunflower oil

450 g/1 lb fresh beef mince

1 small onion, chopped

1/2 green pepper, deseeded and
    chopped

325 g/11½ oz canned sweetcorn
    kernels, drained

200 g/7 oz canned tomatoes

2 tsp chopped fresh thyme

300 ml/10 fl oz beef stock or 1 beef
    stock cube dissolved in
    300 ml/10 fl oz boiling water

salt and pepper

fresh thyme sprigs, to garnish

1 Heat the oil in a heavy-based saucepan. Add the beef. Cook over a medium heat, stirring, for 5 minutes, or until broken up and browned. Drain off any excess fat.

2 Add the onion, pepper, sweetcorn, tomatoes and their juices and chopped thyme. Pour in the stock and bring the mixture to the boil, stirring constantly.

3 Reduce the heat, cover and simmer for 50 minutes. Season to taste with salt and pepper, garnish with fresh thyme sprigs and serve immediately.

# daube of beef

## serves six

350 ml/12 fl oz dry white wine

2 tbsp brandy

1 tbsp white wine vinegar

4 shallots, sliced

4 carrots, sliced

1 garlic clove, finely chopped

6 black peppercorns

4 fresh thyme sprigs

1 fresh rosemary sprig

2 fresh parsley sprigs, plus

    extra to garnish

1 bay leaf

salt

750 g/1 lb 10 oz beef topside, cut

    into 2.5-cm/1-inch cubes

2 tbsp olive oil

800 g/1 lb 12 oz canned

    chopped tomatoes

225 g/8 oz mushrooms, sliced

strip of finely pared orange rind

55 g/2 oz Bayonne ham, cut into

    strips

12 black olives

---

### VARIATION

Bayonne ham is a dry-cured,
smoked ham from the Basses-
Pyrénées. If it is not available,
substitute Parma ham.

---

1 Combine the wine, brandy, vinegar, shallots, carrots, garlic, peppercorns, thyme, rosemary, parsley and bay leaf and season to taste with salt. Add the beef, stirring to coat, then cover with clingfilm and leave in the refrigerator to marinate for 8 hours, or overnight.

2 Preheat the oven to 150°C/300°F/ Gas Mark 2. Drain the beef, reserving the marinade, and pat dry on kitchen paper. Heat half the oil in a large, flameproof casserole. Add the beef in batches and cook over a medium heat, stirring, for 3–4 minutes, or until browned. Transfer the beef to a plate with a slotted spoon. Brown the remaining beef, adding more oil, if necessary.

3 Return all of the beef to the casserole and add the tomatoes and their juices, mushrooms and orange rind. Sieve the reserved marinade into the casserole. Bring to the boil, cover and cook in the oven for 2½ hours.

4 Remove the casserole from the oven, add the ham and olives and return it to the oven to cook for a further 30 minutes, or until the beef is very tender. Discard the orange rind and serve straight from the casserole, garnished with parsley.

# beef goulash

## serves four

2 tbsp vegetable oil

1 large onion, chopped

1 garlic clove, crushed

750 g/1 lb 10 oz lean stewing steak

2 tbsp paprika

425 g/15 oz canned chopped
   tomatoes

2 tbsp tomato purée

1 large red pepper, deseeded
   and chopped

175 g/6 oz mushrooms, sliced

600 ml/1 pint beef stock

1 tbsp cornflour

1 tbsp water

salt and pepper

chopped fresh parsley, to garnish

long-grain rice and wild rice,
   to serve

---

### VARIATION

To make a side dressing of
yogurt, place 4 tablespoons of
natural yogurt in a serving bowl,
sprinkle with a little paprika and
serve with the goulash.

---

1 Heat the vegetable oil in a large, heavy-based frying pan. Add the onion and garlic and cook over a low heat for 3–4 minutes.

2 Using a sharp knife, cut the steak into chunks, add to the frying pan and cook over a high heat for 3 minutes, or until browned. Add the paprika and stir well, then add the tomatoes, tomato purée, red pepper and mushrooms. Cook for a further 2 minutes, stirring frequently. Pour in the stock. Bring to the boil, reduce the heat, cover and simmer for 1½–2 hours, or until the meat is tender.

3 Blend the cornflour and water together in a small bowl, then add to the frying pan, stirring, until thickened and smooth. Cook for 1 minute. Season to taste with salt and pepper.

4 Transfer the beef goulash to a warmed serving dish, garnish with chopped fresh parsley and serve with a mix of long-grain and wild rice.

# stifado

## serves six

450 g/1 lb tomatoes, peeled

150 ml/5 fl oz beef stock

2 tbsp olive oil

450 g/1 lb shallots, peeled

2 garlic cloves, finely chopped

700 g/1 lb 9 oz stewing steak,
cut into 2.5-cm/1-inch cubes

1 fresh rosemary sprig

1 bay leaf

2 tbsp red wine vinegar

salt and pepper

450 g/1 lb potatoes, quartered

**1** Place the tomatoes in a blender or food processor, add the stock and process to a purée. Alternatively, push them through a sieve into a bowl with the back of a wooden spoon and mix with the stock.

**2** Heat the oil in a large, heavy-based saucepan or flameproof casserole. Add the shallots and garlic and cook over a low heat, stirring occasionally, for 8 minutes, or until golden. Transfer to a plate with a slotted spoon. Add the steak to the saucepan and cook, stirring frequently, for 5–8 minutes, or until browned.

**3** Return the shallots and garlic to the saucepan, add the tomato mixture, herbs and vinegar and season to taste with salt and pepper. Cover and simmer gently for 1½ hours. Add the potatoes, re-cover and simmer for a further 30 minutes. Remove and discard the rosemary and bay leaf and serve.

### VARIATION
If you want to prepare this stew quickly, without making a stock, substitute water for the beef stock.

# potato, beef & peanut pot

## serves four

1 tbsp vegetable oil

5 tbsp butter

450 g/1 lb lean beef steak, cut into
    thin strips

1 onion, halved and sliced

2 garlic cloves, crushed

600 g/1 lb 5 oz waxy
    potatoes, diced

½ tsp paprika

4 tbsp crunchy peanut butter

600 ml/1 pint beef stock

25 g/1 oz unsalted peanuts

2 tsp light soy sauce

50 g/1¾ oz sugar snap peas

1 red pepper, deseeded and cut
    into strips

fresh parsley sprigs, to garnish

1 Heat the oil and butter in a
  flameproof casserole.

2 Add the beef strips and fry them
  gently for 3–4 minutes, stirring
and turning the meat until it is sealed
on all sides.

3 Add the onion and garlic and
  cook for a further 2 minutes,
stirring constantly.

4 Add the diced potatoes and cook
  for 3–4 minutes, or until they
begin to brown slightly.

5 Stir in the paprika and peanut
  butter, then gradually blend in the
beef stock. Bring the mixture to the
boil, stirring frequently.

6 Finally, add the peanuts, soy sauce,
  sugar snap peas and red pepper.

7 Cover and cook over a low heat
  for 45 minutes, or until the beef is
cooked right through.

8 Garnish the potato, beef and
  peanut pot with fresh parsley if
liked, and serve immediately.

# paprika pork

## serves four

675 g/1 lb 8 oz pork fillet

2 tbsp sunflower oil

25 g/1 oz butter

1 onion, chopped

1 tbsp paprika

25 g/1 oz plain flour

300 ml/10 fl oz chicken stock or

   1 chicken stock cube dissolved in

   300 ml/10 fl oz boiling water

4 tbsp dry sherry

115 g/4 oz mushrooms, sliced

salt and pepper

150 ml/5 fl oz soured cream

1 Cut the pork into 4-cm/ 1½-inch cubes. Heat the oil and butter in a large saucepan. Add the pork and cook over a medium heat, stirring, for 5 minutes, or until browned. Transfer to a plate with a slotted spoon.

2 Add the chopped onion to the saucepan and cook, stirring occasionally, for 5 minutes, or until softened. Stir in the paprika and flour and cook, stirring constantly, for 2 minutes. Gradually stir in the stock and bring to the boil, stirring constantly.

3 Return the pork to the saucepan, add the sherry and sliced mushrooms and season to taste with salt and pepper. Cover and simmer gently for 20 minutes, or until the pork is tender. Stir in the soured cream and serve.

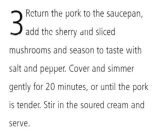

# pot-roast pork

## serves four

1 tbsp sunflower oil

55 g/2 oz butter

1 kg/2 lb 4 oz boned and
  rolled pork loin joint

4 shallots, chopped

6 juniper berries

2 fresh thyme sprigs, plus
  extra to garnish

150 ml/5 fl oz dry cider

150 ml/5 fl oz chicken stock or
  water

salt and pepper

8 celery sticks, chopped

2 tbsp plain flour

150 ml/5 fl oz double cream

freshly cooked peas, to serve

---

**VARIATION**

Substitute 2 thinly sliced fennel
bulbs for the chopped celery if
you would prefer an aniseed
flavour in this dish.

---

1 Heat the oil with half the butter in a heavy-based saucepan or flameproof casserole. Add the pork and cook over a medium heat, turning frequently, for 5–10 minutes, or until browned. Transfer to a plate.

2 Add the shallots to the saucepan and cook, stirring frequently, for 5 minutes, or until softened. Add the juniper berries and thyme sprigs and return the pork to the saucepan, with any juices that have collected on the plate. Pour in the cider and stock, season to taste with salt and pepper, then cover and simmer for 30 minutes. Turn the pork over and add the celery. Re-cover the pan and cook for a further 40 minutes.

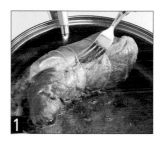

3 Meanwhile, make a beurre manié by mashing the remaining butter with the flour in a small bowl. Transfer the pork and celery to a platter with a slotted spoon and keep warm. Remove and discard the juniper berries and thyme. Whisk the beurre manié, a little at a time, into the simmering cooking liquid. Cook, stirring constantly, for 2 minutes, then stir in the cream and

bring to the boil. Slice the pork and spoon a little of the sauce over it. Garnish with thyme sprigs and serve immediately with the celery and freshly cooked peas. Hand the remaining sauce separately.

# pork hotpot

## serves six

85 g/3 oz plain flour

salt and pepper

1.3 kg/3 lb pork fillet, cut
   into 5-mm/1/4-inch slices

4 tbsp sunflower oil

2 onions, thinly sliced

2 garlic cloves

400 g/14 oz canned chopped
   tomatoes

350 ml/12 fl oz dry white wine

1 tbsp torn fresh basil leaves

2 tbsp chopped fresh parsley

fresh parsley sprigs, to garnish

fresh crusty bread, to serve

or until browned all over. Transfer the
pork to a plate with a slotted spoon.

1 Spread the flour on a plate and
season with salt and pepper. Coat
the pork slices in the flour, shaking off
any excess. Heat the sunflower oil in a
flameproof casserole. Add the pork
slices and cook over a medium heat,
turning occasionally, for 4–5 minutes,

2 Add the onion slices to the
casserole and cook over a low heat,
stirring occasionally, for 10 minutes, or
until golden brown. Finely chop the
garlic, add it to the pan and cook for a
further 2 minutes, then add the
tomatoes, wine and basil leaves and
season to taste with salt and pepper.
Cook, stirring frequently, for 3 minutes.

### VARIATION

Substitute 6 peeled, deseeded
and chopped fresh tomatoes for
the canned ones, adding them
with the wine in Step 2.

3 Return the pork to the casserole,
cover and simmer gently for 1
hour, or until the meat is tender. Snip
in the parsley and serve immediately,
garnished with parsley sprigs, with
fresh crusty bread.

# spicy sausage with lentils

## serves four

1 tbsp sunflower oil

225 g/8 oz spicy sausages, sliced

115 g/4 oz rindless smoked
  bacon, chopped

1 onion, chopped

6 tbsp passata

425 ml/15 fl oz beef stock

600 g/1 lb 5 oz canned lentils,
  drained and rinsed

1/2 tsp paprika

2 tsp red wine vinegar

salt and pepper

fresh thyme sprigs, to garnish

**1** Heat the oil in a large, heavy-based saucepan. Add the sausages and bacon and cook over a medium heat, stirring, for 5 minutes, or until the bacon begins to crisp. Transfer to a plate with a slotted spoon.

**2** Add the chopped onion to the saucepan and cook, stirring occasionally, for 5 minutes, or until softened. Stir in the passata and add the stock and lentils. Reduce the heat, cover and simmer for 10 minutes.

> **VARIATION**
> You can substitute other canned pulses for the lentils, and to turn this into a fish dish, use smoked mackerel instead of the sausages.

**3** Return the sausage slices and bacon to the saucepan, stir in the paprika and red wine vinegar and season to taste with salt and pepper. Heat the mixture through gently for a few minutes, then serve immediately, garnished with fresh thyme sprigs.

57

# basque pork & beans

## serves four

200 g/7 oz dried cannellini beans,
    soaked overnight in enough
    cold water to cover
2 tbsp olive oil, for frying
600 g/1 lb 5 oz boneless leg of
    pork, cut into 5-cm/2-inch chunks
1 large onion, sliced
3 large garlic cloves, crushed
400 g/14 oz canned chopped
    tomatoes
2 green peppers, deseeded and
    sliced
finely grated rind of 1 large orange
salt and pepper
finely chopped fresh parsley,
    to garnish

1 Preheat the oven to 180°C/350°F/
Gas Mark 4. Drain the beans and
place in a large saucepan with fresh
water to cover. Bring to the boil and
boil rapidly for 10 minutes. Reduce the
heat and simmer for 20 minutes. Drain
and reserve.

2 Add enough olive oil to a large,
heavy-based frying pan to cover
the base in a very thin layer. Add the
pork, in batches, and cook over a
medium heat, turning, until browned all
over. Remove from the pan and reserve.
Repeat with the remaining pork.

3 Add more oil to the frying pan, if
necessary, then add the onion
slices and cook over a low heat for
3 minutes. Stir in the garlic and cook
for a further 2 minutes. Return the pork
to the frying pan.

4 Add the tomatoes and bring to the
boil. Reduce the heat, then stir in
the pepper slices, orange rind and
drained beans. Season to taste with
salt and pepper, then transfer the
contents of the frying pan to a large
casserole. Cover the casserole and
cook in the preheated oven for 45
minutes, or until the beans and pork
are tender. Serve immediately, straight
from the casserole, sprinkled with
chopped parsley.

---

### VARIATION

Add sliced and fried chorizo
sausage for a spicier dish.
Leftover beans and peppers can
be used in a pasta sauce.

---

# roasted seafood

## serves four

600 g/1 lb 5 oz new potatoes

3 red onions, cut into wedges

2 courgettes, cut into chunks

8 garlic cloves

2 lemons, cut into wedges

4 fresh rosemary sprigs

4 tbsp olive oil

350 g/12 oz unpeeled prawns,
    preferably raw

2 small prepared squid, chopped
    into rings

4 tomatoes, quartered

---

### VARIATION

Most vegetables are suitable for
roasting in the oven. Try adding
450 g/1 lb pumpkin, squash or
aubergine, if you prefer.

---

1 Scrub the potatoes to remove any dirt. Cut any large potatoes in half. Place the potatoes in a large roasting tin, together with the onions, courgettes, garlic, lemon wedges and rosemary sprigs.

2 Pour the oil into the roasting tin and toss to coat the vegetables. Cook in a preheated oven, 200°C/400°F/Gas Mark 6, for 40 minutes, turning occasionally, until the potatoes are cooked and tender.

3 Once the potatoes are tender, add the prawns, squid rings and tomato quarters, tossing gently to coat in the hot oil, and roast for 10 minutes. All of the vegetables should be cooked through and slightly charred for full flavour, and all the prawns should have turned pink.

4 Transfer the roasted seafood and vegetables to warmed serving plates using a slotted spoon, and serve immediately.

# aromatic seafood rice

## serves four

225 g/8 oz basmati rice

2 tbsp ghee or vegetable oil

1 onion, chopped

1 garlic clove, crushed

1 tsp cumin seeds

½–1 tsp chilli powder

4 cloves

1 cinnamon stick or piece of
    cassia bark

2 tsp curry paste

225 g/8 oz peeled prawns

500g/1 lb 2 oz white fish fillets
    (such as monkfish, cod or
    haddock), skinned and boned
    and cut into bite-sized pieces

600 ml/1 pint boiling water

55 g/2 oz frozen peas

55 g/2 oz frozen sweetcorn kernels

1–2 tbsp lime juice

2 tbsp toasted desiccated coconut

salt and pepper

TO GARNISH

1 fresh coriander sprig

slices of lime

1 Put the rice into a sieve and wash well under cold running water until the water runs clear. Drain well.

2 Heat the ghee or oil in a large pan over a low heat. Add the onion, garlic, spices and curry paste and fry very gently for 1 minute.

3 Stir in the rice and mix well until coated in the spiced oil. Add the prawns and white fish. Season well with salt and pepper. Stir lightly, then pour in the boiling water.

4 Cover and cook gently for about 10 minutes. Add the peas and sweetcorn, cover and cook for a further 8 minutes. Remove from the heat and leave to stand for 10 minutes.

5 Uncover the pan, fluff up the rice with a fork and transfer to a large, warmed serving platter.

6 Sprinkle the dish with the lime juice and toasted coconut and garnish with a coriander sprig and 2 lime slices. Serve immediately.

# indian cod with tomatoes

## serves four

3 tbsp vegetable oil

4 cod steaks, 2.5-cm/1-inch thick

1 onion, chopped finely

2 garlic cloves, crushed

1 red pepper, deseeded
   and chopped

1 tsp ground coriander

1 tsp ground cumin

1 tsp turmeric

½ tsp garam masala

400 g/14 oz canned
   chopped tomatoes

150 ml/5 fl oz coconut milk

1 2 tbsp chopped fresh coriander
   or parsley

salt and pepper

1 Heat the oil in a frying pan over a medium heat. Add the fish and season with salt and pepper. Fry until browned on both sides, but not cooked through. Remove and reserve.

2 Add the onion, garlic, red pepper and spices and cook gently over a low heat for 2 minutes, stirring frequently. Add the tomatoes, bring to the boil and simmer for 5 minutes.

3 Add the fish to the pan and simmer gently for 8 minutes, or until the fish is cooked through.

4 Remove the fish from the pan and keep warm in a serving dish. Add the coconut milk and chopped coriander to the pan and heat gently.

5 Spoon the sauce over the fish and serve immediately

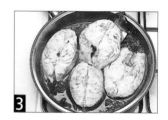

# vermicelli & vegetable flan

## serves four

6 tbsp butter, plus extra for greasing

225 g/8 oz dried vermicelli
  or spaghetti

1 tbsp olive oil

1 onion, chopped

140 g/5 oz button mushrooms

1 green pepper, deseeded and
  sliced into thin rings

150 ml/5 fl oz milk

3 eggs, lightly beaten

2 tbsp double cream

1 tsp dried oregano

freshly grated nutmeg

15 g/½ oz freshly grated
  Parmesan cheese

salt and pepper

tomato and basil salad,
  to serve (optional)

1 Generously grease a 20-cm/
8-inch loose-bottomed flan tin
with a little butter.

2 Bring a large saucepan of lightly
salted water to the boil. Add the
vermicelli or spaghetti and olive oil,
bring back to the boil and cook for 8–10
minutes, until tender but still firm to the
bite. Drain, return to the saucepan, add
2 tablespoons of the butter and shake
the saucepan to coat the pasta.

3 Press the pasta on to the base
and around the sides of the flan
tin to make a flan case.

4 Melt the remaining butter in a
large frying pan over a medium
heat. Add the chopped onion and cook
over a low heat, stirring occasionally,
until translucent.

5 Add the mushrooms and pepper
rings to the frying pan and cook,
stirring, for 2–3 minutes. Spoon the
onion, mushroom and pepper mixture
into the flan case and press it evenly
into the base.

6 Beat together the milk, eggs and
cream, stir in the oregano and
season to taste with nutmeg and
pepper. Carefully pour the mixture over
the vegetables, then sprinkle with the
Parmesan cheese.

7 Bake the flan in a preheated
oven, 180°C/350°F/Gas Mark 4,
for about 40–45 minutes, or until the
filling has set.

8 Carefully slide the flan out of the
tin and serve warm with a tomato
and basil salad, if you wish.

# italian fish stew

## serves four

2 tbsp olive oil

2 red onions, chopped finely

1 garlic clove, crushed

2 courgettes, sliced

400 g/14 oz canned
   chopped tomatoes

850 ml/1½ pints fish or
   vegetable stock

85 g/3 oz small, dried pasta shapes

350 g/12 oz firm white fish, such
   as cod, haddock or hake

1 tbsp chopped fresh basil or
   oregano or 1 tsp dried oregano

1 tsp grated lemon rind

1 tbsp cornflour

1 tbsp water

salt and pepper

4 fresh basil or oregano sprigs,
   to garnish

1 Heat the oil in a large pan over a low heat. Add the onions and garlic and cook, stirring occasionally, for about 5 minutes until softened. Add the courgettes and cook, stirring frequently, for 2–3 minutes.

2 Add the tomatoes and stock to the pan and bring to the boil over a medium heat. Add the pasta, bring back to the boil, then reduce the heat and cover. Simmer for 5 minutes.

3 Skin and bone the fish, then cut it into chunks. Add to the pan with the basil or oregano and lemon rind and simmer gently for 5 minutes until the fish is opaque and flakes easily (take care not to overcook it) and the pasta is tender, but still firm to the bite.

4 Blend the cornflour with the water to form a smooth paste and stir into the stew. Cook for 2 minutes,

stirring constantly, until thickened. Season to taste with salt and pepper.

5 Ladle the stew into 4 large, warmed soup bowls. Garnish with fresh basil or oregano sprigs and serve immediately.

# rice & peas

## serves four

1 tbsp olive oil

4 tbsp butter

55 g/2 oz pancetta or streaky
  bacon, chopped

1 small onion, chopped

1.4 litres/2½ pints hot chicken stock

225 g/8 oz frozen or canned
  petits pois

200 g/7 oz risotto rice

3 tbsp chopped fresh parsley

55 g/2 oz freshly grated
  Parmesan cheese

pepper

1 Heat the oil and half of the butter in a large pan over a low heat. Add the pancetta or bacon and onion and cook, stirring occasionally, for 5 minutes, or until the onion is translucent but not browned.

2 Add the stock to the pan and bring to the boil over a medium heat. Stir in the rice and season with pepper to taste. Bring to the boil, reduce the heat and simmer, stirring occasionally, for about 20–30 minutes or until the rice is tender.

3 Add the chopped parsley and the petits pois and cook for 8 minutes or until the petits pois are heated through. Stir in the remaining butter and the grated Parmesan cheese.

4 Transfer the risotto to a large, warmed serving dish and serve immediately with pepper.

# milanese risotto

## serves four

2 good pinches of saffron threads

85 g/3 oz butter

1 large onion, chopped finely

1–2 garlic cloves, crushed

350 g/12 oz arborio rice

150 ml/5 fl oz dry white wine

1.2 litres/2 pints boiling
   vegetable stock

85 g/3 oz freshly grated
   Parmesan cheese

salt and pepper

1 Put the saffron into a small bowl, cover with 3–4 tablespoons of almost boiling water and leave to soak while you prepare the risotto.

2 Melt 55 g/2 oz of the butter in a pan over a low heat. Add the onion and garlic and fry until soft but not coloured. Add the rice and cook for 2–3 minutes, or until the grains are coated in oil and starting to colour.

3 Add the wine to the rice and simmer gently, stirring from time to time, until it is all absorbed.

4 Add a ladleful (150 ml/5 fl oz) of the hot stock. Cook, stirring constantly, until the liquid is absorbed before adding more.

5 When all the stock has been absorbed (this should take about 20 minutes), the rice should be tender but not soft and soggy. Add the saffron liquid, Parmesan cheese and remaining butter. Season to taste with salt and pepper and simmer for 2 minutes until piping hot and thoroughly mixed.

6 Cover the pan tightly and leave to stand for 5 minutes off the heat. Give a good stir and serve immediately.

# sun-dried risotto

## serves six

about 12 sun-dried tomatoes,
  not in oil
2 tbsp olive oil
1 large onion, chopped finely
4–6 garlic cloves, chopped finely
400 g/14 oz arborio or carnaroli rice
1.5 litres/2¾ pints chicken or
  vegetable stock, simmering
115 g/4 oz frozen peas, thawed
2 tbsp chopped fresh
  flat-leaf parsley
115 g/4 oz freshly grated aged
  pecorino cheese
1 tbsp extra virgin olive oil

1 Put the sun-dried tomatoes into a bowl and pour over enough boiling water to cover. Stand for about 30 minutes or until soft and supple. Drain and pat dry with kitchen paper, then shred thinly and reserve.

2 Heat the oil in a frying pan over a medium heat. Add the onion and cook for 2 minutes until starting to soften. Add the garlic and cook for 15 seconds. Add the rice and cook, stirring, for 2 minutes, or until the rice is translucent and coated with oil.

3 Add a ladleful of the hot stock, which will bubble and steam rapidly. Cook gently, stirring constantly, until the liquid is absorbed.

4 Continue adding the stock, about half a ladleful at a time, letting each addition be absorbed by the rice before adding the next.

5 After about 15 minutes, stir in the sun-dried tomatoes. Continue to cook, adding the stock, until the rice is tender, but firm to the bite. Add the peas with the last addition of stock.

6 Remove from the heat and stir in the parsley and half the cheese. Cover, leave to stand for 1 minute, then spoon into 6 dishes. The risotto should have a creamy consistency. Drizzle with oil and sprinkle with the remaining cheese. Serve immediately.

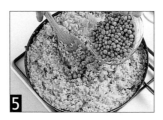

# green risotto

## serves four

1 onion, chopped

2 tbsp olive oil

225 g/8 oz risotto rice

700 ml/1¼ pints hot vegetable stock

350 g/12 oz mixed green
vegetables, such as asparagus,
fine green beans, mangetout,
courgettes, broccoli florets,
frozen peas

2 tbsp chopped fresh parsley

55 g/2 oz Parmesan
cheese shavings

salt and pepper

### COOK'S TIP

For extra texture, stir in
a few toasted pine kernels
or coarsely chopped cashew
nuts at the end of the
cooking time.

1 Put the onion and oil into a large
bowl. Cover and cook in the
microwave on HIGH for 2 minutes.

2 Add the rice and stir until coated
thoroughly in the oil. Pour in
about 5 tablespoons of the hot stock.
Cook, uncovered, for 2 minutes, until
the liquid is absorbed. Pour in another
5 tablespoons of the stock and cook,
uncovered, on HIGH for 2 minutes.
Repeat once more.

3 Chop or slice the vegetables into
even sized pieces. Stir into the
rice with the remaining stock. Cover
and cook on HIGH for 8 minutes,
stirring occasionally, until most of the
liquid has been absorbed and the rice
is just tender.

4 Stir in the chopped parsley and
season with salt and pepper.
Leave to stand, covered, for 5 minutes.
The rice should be tender and creamy.

5 Transfer to a large serving dish
and scatter the Parmesan cheese
over the risotto before serving.

# potato & cauliflower curry

## serves four

150 ml/5 fl oz vegetable oil

½ tsp white cumin seeds

4 dried red chillies

2 onions, sliced

1 tsp finely chopped fresh
    root ginger

1 tsp crushed garlic

1 tsp chilli powder

1 tsp salt

pinch of ground turmeric

675 g/1 lb 8 oz potatoes, chopped

½ cauliflower, cut into small florets

2 fresh green chillies (optional)

1 tbsp fresh coriander leaves

150 ml/5 fl oz water

### COOK'S TIP

Ground ginger is no substitute
for the fresh root. It is less
aromatic and flavoursome and
cannot be used in fried or
sautéed dishes, because it
burns easily at the high
temperatures required.

1 Heat the oil in a large, heavy-based saucepan. Add the white cumin seeds and dried red chillies to the pan, stirring to mix.

2 Add the onions to the pan and fry over a medium heat, stirring occasionally, for about 5–8 minutes, until golden brown.

3 Mix the ginger, garlic, chilli powder, salt and turmeric together. Add the spice mixture to the onions and stir-fry for about 2 minutes.

4 Add the potatoes and cauliflower to the pan and stir to coat thoroughly with the spice mixture. Reduce the heat and add the green chillies (if using), coriander leaves and water to the pan. Cover and simmer for about 10–15 minutes, until the vegetables are cooked right through and are tender.

5 Transfer the potato and cauliflower curry to warmed serving plates and serve immediately.

# mixed vegetables

## serves four

300 ml/10 fl oz vegetable oil

1 tsp mustard seeds

1 tsp onion seeds

½ tsp white cumin seeds

3–4 curry leaves, chopped

450 g/1 lb onions, chopped finely

3 tomatoes, chopped

½ red and ½ green pepper, deseeded and sliced

1 tsp finely chopped fresh root ginger

1 tsp crushed garlic

1 tsp chilli powder

¼ tsp ground turmeric

1 tsp salt

425 ml/15 fl oz water

450 g/1 lb potatoes, cut into pieces

½ cauliflower, cut into small florets

4 carrots, peeled and sliced

3 fresh green chillies, deseeded and chopped finely

1 tbsp fresh coriander leaves

1 tbsp lemon juice

1 Heat the oil in a large saucepan. Add the mustard, onion and white cumin seeds along with the curry leaves and fry until they turn a shade darker.

2 Add the onions to the pan and fry over a medium heat until golden brown.

3 Add the tomatoes and red and green peppers and stir-fry for about 5 minutes.

4 Add the ginger, garlic, chilli powder, turmeric and salt and mix well.

5 Add 300 ml/10 fl oz of the water, cover and simmer for about 10–12 minutes, stirring occasionally.

6 Add the potatoes, cauliflower, carrots, green chillies and coriander leaves and stir-fry for about 5 minutes.

7 Add the remaining water and the lemon juice, stirring to combine. Cover and simmer for about 15 minutes, stirring occasionally.

8 Transfer the mixed vegetables to warmed serving plates and serve immediately.

# chickpea curry

## serves four

6 tbsp vegetable oil

2 onions, sliced

1 tsp finely chopped fresh
    root ginger

1 tsp ground cumin

1 tsp ground coriander

1 tsp fresh garlic, crushed

1 tsp chilli powder

2 fresh green chillies

1 tbsp fresh coriander leaves

150 ml/5 fl oz water

300 g/10½ oz potatoes

400 g/14 oz canned chickpeas,
    drained and rinsed

1 tbsp lemon or lime juice

chapatis, to serve (optional)

1 Heat the oil in a large saucepan over a medium heat.

2 Add the onions to the pan and fry, stirring occasionally, until they are golden brown.

3 Reduce the heat, add the ginger, ground cumin, ground coriander, garlic, chilli powder, fresh green chillies and fresh coriander leaves to the pan and stir-fry for 2 minutes.

4 Add the water to the mixture in the pan and stir to mix.

5 Using a sharp knife, cut the potatoes into small cubes.

6 Add the potatoes and chickpeas to the mixture in the pan, cover and simmer, stirring occasionally, for 5–7 minutes.

7 Sprinkle the lemon or lime juice over the curry.

8 Transfer the chickpea curry to serving dishes. Serve the curry hot with chapatis, if you wish.

# potato & vegetable curry

## serves four

4 tbsp vegetable oil

675 g/1½ lb waxy potatoes, cut into
large chunks

2 onions, quartered

3 garlic cloves, crushed

1 tsp garam masala

½ tsp ground turmeric

½ tsp ground cumin

½ tsp ground coriander

2 tsp grated fresh root ginger

1 fresh red chilli, deseeded
and chopped

225 g/8 oz cauliflower florets

4 tomatoes, skinned and quartered

75 g/2¾ oz frozen peas

2 tbsp chopped fresh coriander

300 ml10 fl oz vegetable stock

shredded fresh coriander,
to garnish

boiled rice or Indian bread, to serve

### COOK'S TIP

Use a large heavy-based
saucepan or frying pan for this
recipe to ensure that the
potatoes are cooked thoroughly.

1 Heat the vegetable oil in a large heavy-based saucepan or frying pan. Add the potato chunks, onions and garlic and fry over a low heat, stirring frequently, for 2–3 minutes.

2 Add the garam masala, turmeric, ground cumin, ground coriander, ginger and chilli to the pan, mixing the spices into the vegetables. Fry over a low heat, stirring constantly, for 1 minute.

3 Add the cauliflower florets, tomato quarters, peas and chopped coriander to the curry mixture and stir well. Pour in the vegetable stock and stir again.

4 Cook the potato curry over a low heat for 30–40 minutes, or until the potatoes are tender and completely cooked through.

5 Garnish the potato curry with fresh coriander and serve with plain boiled rice or warm Indian bread.

This is a Parragon Book
This edition published in 2004

Parragon
Queen Street House
4 Queen Street
Bath BA1 1HE, UK

ISBN: 1-40544-023-6

Printed in China
Produced by the Bridgewater Company Ltd

NOTE

This book also uses imperial and metric measurements. Follow the same units
of measurement throughout; do not mix imperial and metric.
All spoon measurements are level: teaspoons are assumed to be 5 ml and
tablespoons are assumed to be 15 ml. Unless otherwise stated, milk is assumed
to be whole milk, eggs and individual vegetables such as potatoes are medium,
and pepper is freshly ground black pepper.

The times given for each recipe are an approximate guide only because the
preparation times may differ according to the techniques used by different
people and the cooking times may vary as a result of the type of oven used.

Recipes using raw or very lightly cooked eggs should be
avoided by infants, the elderly, pregnant women, convalescents, and anyone
suffering from an illness.